THIS BOOK BELONGS TO

. . . .

THANK YOU FOR BEING OUR VALUED CUSTOMER. WE WOULD BE GRATEFUL IF YOU SHARED THIS HAPPY EXPERIENCE ON AMAZON.

THIS HELPS US TO CONTINUE PROVIDING GREAT PRODUCTS, AND HELPS POTENTIAL BUYERS TO MAKE CONFIDENT DECISIONS

COLOR TEST PAGE

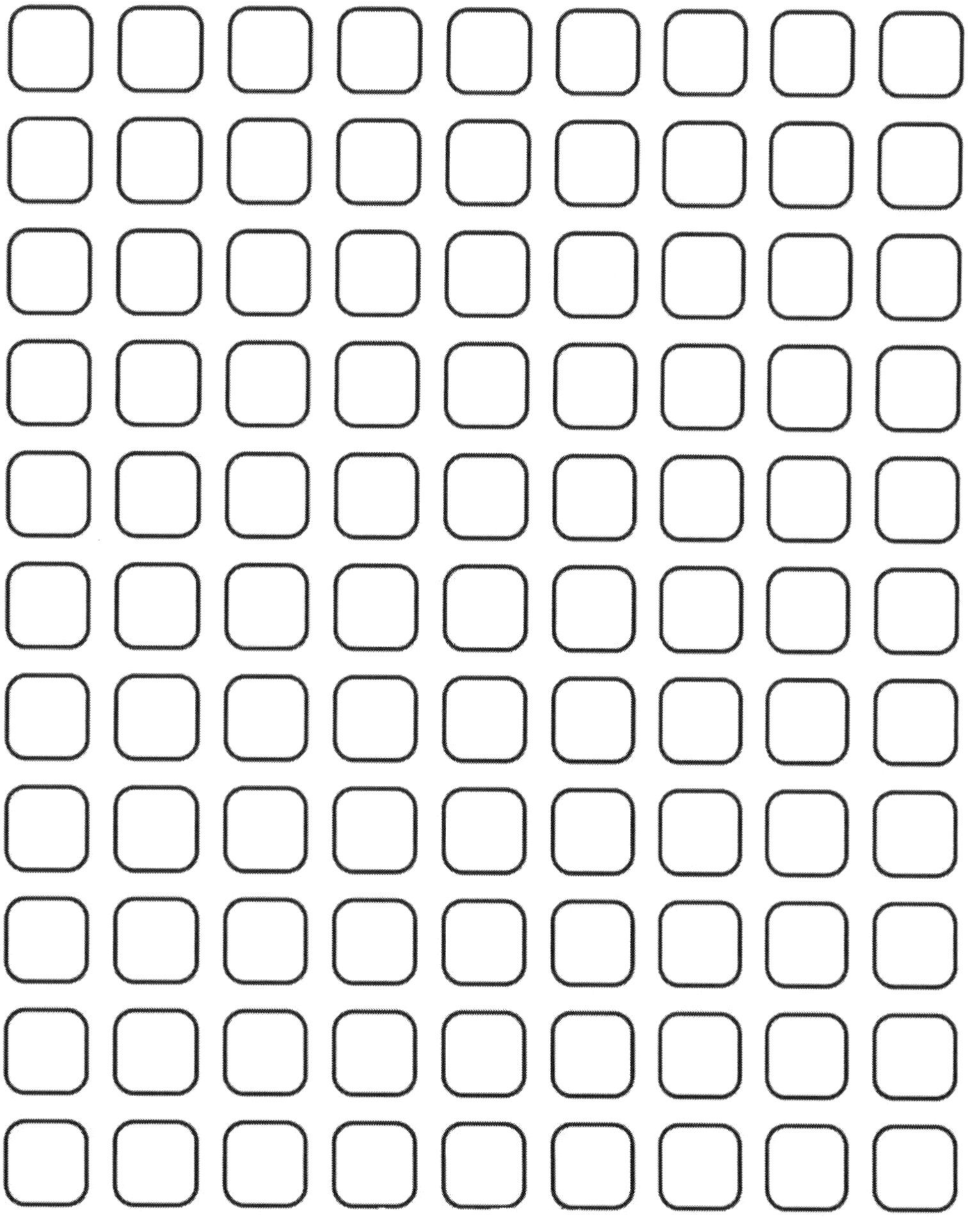

Freedom

Black
Girl Magic

No Justice
No Peace

Equality

Freedom

WE WANT
Justice

Peace
be Still

Supreme

L
N

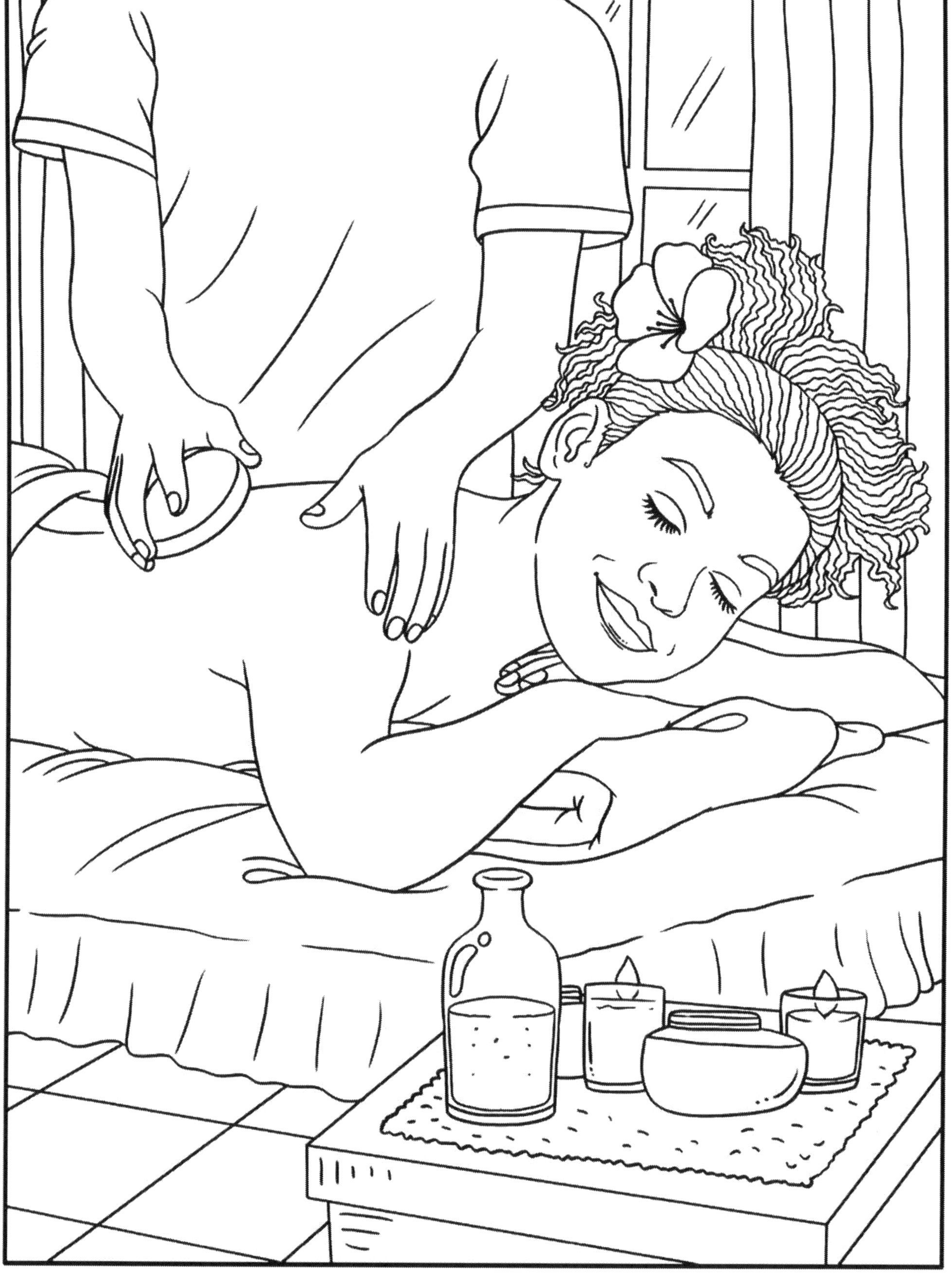

BLACK
GIRL MAGIC

Made in the USA
Columbia, SC
15 March 2022

57722943R00059